Troy Polamalu

by Michael Sandler

Consultant: James Alder
Football Expert
football.about.com

New York, New York

Credits

Cover and Title Page, © Schott Halleran/Getty Images; 4, © AP Photo/Ed Reinke; 5, © Larry French/Getty Images; 6, © AP Photo/David Drapkin; 7, © Rob Tringali/SportsChrome/Getty Images; 9, Courtesy of Singleton Park/Douglas County Parks; 10, © Tom Hanck/Icon SMI/Newscom; 11, © Stephen Dunn/Getty Images; 12, © Gary Hershorn/Reuters/Landov; 13, © AP Photo/Amy Sancetta; 14, © Michael Fabus/Getty Images; 15, © Mike Fabus/NFL/WireImage/Getty Images; 16, © Bunting Graphics, Inc.; 17, © Tony Medina/Icon SMI/Newscom; 18, © AP Photo/Mike Fabus; 19, © Operation Once in a Lifetime; 20, © John G. Mabanglo/EPA/Corbis; 21, © AP Photo/Keith Srakocic; 22L, © KRT/Newscom; 22R, © Jason Pohuski/CSM/Landov.

Publisher: Kenn Goin
Senior Editor: Lisa Wiseman
Creative Director: Spencer Brinker
Photo Researcher: Picture Perfect Professionals, LLC
Design: Dawn Beard Creative

Library of Congress Cataloging-in-Publication Data

Sandler, Michael, 1965–
   Troy Polamalu / by Michael Sandler.
      p. cm. — (Football heroes making a difference)
   Includes bibliographical references and index.
   ISBN-13: 978-1-61772-312-4 (library binding)
   ISBN-10: 1-61772-312-6 (library binding)
   1. Polamalu, Troy, 1981–Juvenile literature. 2. Football players—United States—Biography—Juvenile literature. I. Title.
   GV939.P65S36 2012
   796.33092—dc22
   [B]
                                         2011011675

For more information, write to Bearport Publishing Company, Inc., 45 West 21st Street, Suite 3B, New York, New York 10010. Printed in the United States of America.

10 9 8 7 6 5 4 3 2

CONTENTS

Turning to Troy

A meeting between the Pittsburgh Steelers and the Baltimore Ravens was always a battle between tough, bruising defensive teams. The game on December 5, 2010, was no different.

Both teams desperately wanted a victory. The winner would take first place in the **AFC North**. The losing team would drop into second place.

With fewer than five minutes left to play, a 10–6 lead, and **possession** of the ball, Baltimore quarterback Joe Flacco had his team close to victory. To turn this game around, Pittsburgh needed a big defensive play. So they looked to **safety** Troy Polamalu—one of the NFL's greatest **defenders**.

Troy Polamalu in action

The Steelers (right) and the Ravens (left) played in Baltimore on December 5, 2010. At the time, the two teams were tied for first place with 8–3 records.

With Troy's help, Pittsburgh had the NFL's best defense in 2010–2011. The Steelers allowed just 63 **rushing yards** (58 m) and fewer than 15 points a game.

The Game Changer

As Joe Flacco dropped back to throw the ball, Troy exploded across the **line of scrimmage**. He flew like a bullet toward the Baltimore quarterback, swooping in to grab him. As he did, Troy swept his right hand across Joe's throwing arm, knocking the football free. Then Steelers **linebacker** LaMarr Woodley scooped up the bouncing ball and ran all the way downfield to the Baltimore nine-yard (8-m) line. Suddenly, Pittsburgh had the ball right next to the Ravens' **end zone**.

Three plays later, Steelers quarterback Ben Roethlisberger threw a short touchdown pass to **running back** Isaac Redman. Pittsburgh took the lead, and minutes later they had a 13–10 win. As so often happens for the Steelers, a Troy Polamalu play had changed the whole game!

Troy (#43) knocks the ball out of Ravens quarterback Joe Flacco's (#5) hand.

Pittsburgh's win knocked Baltimore out of first place. The Steelers held on to first place through the end of the season and took the 2010–2011 division title.

LaMarr Woodley (#56) runs down the field with the ball after Troy (#43) knocked it out of Joe Flacco's hand.

An Important Move

As a child, Troy had dreamed about becoming a pro football player. At the time, however, doing so seemed unlikely. Troy grew up in a rough neighborhood in the city of Santa Ana, California. Many of the kids who lived there, including his brother and sisters, often got into trouble. Some committed crimes, while others got mixed up in gangs or with drugs.

Troy might have gotten into trouble, too, if not for a summer visit to his aunt and uncle in Tenmile, Oregon, at the age of eight. The small town they lived in was very different from Santa Ana. Instead of getting into trouble, Troy spent his time outdoors fishing and camping. He loved it there so much that he asked his family if he could stay on and go to school. They said yes, and for Troy, a new life began.

Troy lived in Tenmile until he went away to college.

8

Troy enjoyed many outdoor activities while living in Oregon.

Troy and his family are of Samoan **descent**. Samoa is an island country located in the South Pacific Ocean.

Sports Star

Troy thrived in Oregon. At school, he made friends and got good grades. On the athletic field, he was outstanding. By high school, there wasn't a sport Troy hadn't mastered. In soccer, he scored goal after goal. In baseball, he blasted home runs. In basketball, he could dunk against anyone. In football, Troy was simply unstoppable.

Football was the sport he chose to play in college at the University of Southern California (USC). By junior year, Troy was USC's team captain and one of the country's best **defensive backs**. After he finished his senior season, many NFL teams wanted Troy to play for them. The Pittsburgh Steelers chose Troy with the 16th pick in the 2003 NFL draft.

Troy warms up before a USC game.

Troy playing for USC in 2002

At USC, Troy was a two-time **All-American**. As a senior, Troy helped lead his team to a 38–17 win over the University of Iowa in the **Orange Bowl**.

Helping Ways

Troy's success with the Steelers has earned him thousands of fans, but he had plenty of admirers even before arriving in Pittsburgh. Back in Oregon, people respected Troy for more than his football skills. They loved him just as much for his kind heart and helping ways.

As a student at Douglas High School, he had spent much of his free time working and playing with schoolmates who were in a special education program. These kids struggled in school as a result of their **mental disabilities**. Troy taught them how to play different sports. As their friend, Troy enjoyed teaching his schoolmates, and he especially liked seeing the joy it brought to them as they succeeded. "The kids I worked with are like my best friends," Troy said.

Troy (#43) greets fans before a game.

Troy signing autographs
before a Steelers practice

Troy is popular with football fans everywhere, not just in Pittsburgh. In fact, he is so popular that his number 43 jersey was the top-selling NFL jersey in 2010–2011.

Children's Hospital

As an adult, Troy finds that helping other people still brings a smile to his face. It's something he's continued to do since joining the Steelers. One place he likes to spend time is at the Children's Hospital of Pittsburgh of UPMC. There, Troy visits and plays with young patients.

For kids with serious illnesses, a visit from a Super Bowl-winning superstar is a welcome break from their medical treatments. It also provides a big boost to their spirits. One spring, for example, Troy spent time with a teenager named Joe Duffy, who was suffering from kidney problems and **leukemia**. The visit was a hit. Joe "hadn't been out of bed for several days," said his father, "but he got out of bed then."

Troy also helps raise money for the Children's Hospital of Pittsburgh. During one telethon, Troy helped raise more than $140,000 for the hospital.

Troy has developed friendships with many of the kids he's met on hospital visits. Often he sends them text messages or calls them after his football games.

Helping Veterans

Troy also likes helping soldiers who have served in America's wars. In 2007, he and his wife, Theodora, started the Harry Panos **Fund**. Named after Theodora's grandfather, a World War II (1939–1945) **veteran**, the fund was established to help soldiers and their families, particularly soldiers injured in Iraq and Afghanistan. The fund gives money to organizations such as Operation Once in a Lifetime. This group makes the dreams of U.S. soldiers come true in many ways, including helping them get medical care for their families, buying holiday gifts for their children, and purchasing airplane tickets for them to visit their relatives. Troy says, "I believe this is important because they are true American heroes."

Troy with his wife, Theodora, and their son

These soldiers, whose dream to attend a Pittsburgh Steelers game was granted through Operation Once in a Lifetime, visit the team's locker room.

Troy's interest in helping veterans was sparked by a visit to Walter Reed Army Medical Center in Washington, D.C. There, he met several young female veterans who had been injured by bombs. Afterward, he came home and talked to his wife about ways that they could help.

At His Best

Safety is a position where players have to do a little bit of everything. Sometimes Troy defends against deep passes. At other times, he hangs back just behind the line of scrimmage, waiting to tackle running backs. Once in a while, he attacks the quarterback on a **blitz**. Troy performs these tasks as well as or better than any other player in the league.

Still, of the many things that Troy does, his finest actions are probably those he performs off the field. Whether he's working to help soldiers who have made sacrifices for their country, or sitting down to play video games with a sick child in need of a smile, it is Troy Polamalu at his best.

Troy (#43) makes a tackle.

After winning the AFC North title in 2010–2011, Troy and the Pittsburgh Steelers advanced into the Super Bowl for the third time in his career. Pittsburgh fought hard against the Green Bay Packers, but lost the game, 31–25.

The Troy File

Troy is a football hero
on and off the field.
Here are some highlights.

Troy is famous for the long, curly black hair that flows out beneath his helmet. To Troy, long hair reminds him of ancient warriors from the past. Having long hair means he is ready to do battle in a football game.

In 2010, Troy was named to the NFL's All-Decade team, a group of 53 players considered to be the very best in the league from 2000–2009.

In 2010–2011, Troy was named the NFL's Defensive Player of the Year. This is the highest honor a safety can receive. During his great season, he intercepted 7 passes and made 63 tackles, even though he missed two games because of an injury.

Glossary

AFC North (AY-EFF-SEE NORTH) one of the four divisions in the NFL's American Football Conference (AFC)

All-American (*awl*-uh-MER-uh-kuhn) a high school or college athlete who is named one of the best in his or her position in the entire country

All-Pro (*awl*-PROH) a player who is voted one of the best at his position

blitz (BLITS) a play in which the defensive team sends many players to try and tackle the quarterback

defenders (di-FEN-durz) players who have the job of stopping the other team from scoring

defensive backs (di-FEN-siv BAKS) safeties and cornerbacks; defensive players who line up farther behind the line of scrimmage

descent (di-SENT) origin; where a person's family came from

end zone (END ZOHN) the area at either end of a football field where touchdowns are scored

fund (FUHND) money kept to be used for a specific purpose

leukemia (loo-KEE-mee-uh) a serious disease in which a person's blood makes too many white cells

linebacker (LINE-bak-ur) a defensive player who makes tackles and defends passes

line of scrimmage (LINE UHV SKRIM-ij) an imaginary line across the field where the ball is put at the beginning of a play

mental disabilities (MEN-tuhl *diss*-uh-BIL-uh-teez) difficulties with thinking skills and thought processing

Orange Bowl (OR-inj BOHL) a famous college football game held each year in Miami, Florida

possession (puh-ZESH-uhn) when a team has the ball and is trying to score

Pro Bowl (PROH BOHL) the yearly All-Star game for the season's best NFL players

receivers (ri-SEE-vurz) players whose job it is to catch passes

running back (RUHN-ing BAK) a player who carries the ball on running plays

rushing yards (RUHSH-ing YARDZ) yards gained on plays in which the ball is run

safety (SAYF-tee) a defensive player who lines up farther back than other defensive players

veteran (VET-ur-uhn) a person who has served in the military

Bibliography

Mims, Steve. "The Roots of a Hometown HERO." *Register-Guard* (Eugene, OR) (February 1, 2006).

Pucin, Diane. "Spirit of Troy." *Los Angeles Times* (November 21, 2002).

Veltrop, Kyle. "Simply the Best." *Sporting News* (September 1, 2006).

Sports Illustrated Magazine

Read More

Sandler, Michael. *Pro Football's Dream Teams (Football-O-Rama).* New York: Bearport (2011).

Sandler, Michael. *Pro Football's Stars of the Defense (Football-O-Rama).* New York: Bearport (2011).

Sandler, Michael. *Santonio Holmes and the Pittsburgh Steelers: Super Bowl XLIII (Super Bowl Superstars).* New York: Bearport (2010).

Learn More Online

To learn more about Troy Polamalu and the Pittsburgh Steelers, visit
www.bearportpublishing.com/FootballHeroes

Index